Catharsis

Destiny Moore

BookLeaf Publishing
India | USA | UK

Presentation by *BookLeaf Publishing*

Web: www.bookleafpub.com

E-mail: info@bookleafpub.com

ISBN: 978-93-5744-479-8

First edition 2022

PREFACE

For years I have had a love-hate relationship with writing, but ultimately it is something I have always gone back to. I have never been motivated to turn my hobby into a career until now, and this book is my first attempt at taking my writing seriously. I believe there is no coincidence with this timing as this sudden chunk of determination has arrived at a time in my life that I can only describe as turbulent.

Feed Me

We covet wisps of courtesy,
Like morsels for the malnourished
And we bite the hand that feeds us
Yet wail about our empty stomachs

Sing for your supper!
And wolf down the scraps
Of decency and kindness
Before you're back to begging

We are the ravenous masses
And we lie sickly
You are no more hungry than I
Yet why do you get a bigger bite?

The Bloody Thing Won't Light

It's out with the old and in with the same
I've grown comfortable with monotony
But monotony still doesn't feel enough
I am like dynamite on a leash
But when will my fuse light?
I have the kindling of tenacity
But nothing to stoke zeal

I'd ask the lighter for a hand
And request aid from the scissors
But I don't want to waste fluid
Or dull a blade
And I've been burnt before
So I'm wary of the sparks
Perhaps I've leashed myself

Inclement

I open the curtains to let in the light
It's time to repel the dark
But as the drapes fly past
I realise
The sky – it still remains grey

I am not convinced the sun exists
Not when I can see so many clouds
Perhaps the breeze will clear them away
But the breeze has been absent for a while

I'm So Confused

It's all happening
But what?

Do I know?
Do you?

Who's in charge here?
Is it you?

Who do you work for?
Who do I work for?

You won't answer to me?
I won't answer to you

How did I get here?
What's stopping me from leaving?

What is happening?

Speak

And in that moment,
The silence said it all
A room full of emptiness
I did not wish to disrupt the chaos
For it was a wonderful distraction
But the beating in my head bade me to speak
To an audience I did not have
And thus the words tumbled down my face
And I remained unheard

I Waited

You claimed any room you entered
And lifted the atmosphere with your presence
The walls smiled at your arrival
As did I

They frowned as much as I did
Whenever you left
But they never awaited your return like I did,
Willing it over and over

Once more you departed
And I expected your company another day
But that day never came
And the walls never smiled again

You were my favourite person
And now you are my favourite memory

Beholder

Our eyes had not met in so long
It was a reunion I had longed for
Yet I found myself unable to look
Had you grown tired of me?
I never felt big enough to fill your shadow
I just wish I'd known that it never bothered you
Then maybe I could have met your gaze

The Tide

My mind is meandering
Between mirage and matter
I am drunk on limbo
I am not aware of my consciousness
Or even an unconsciousness

I am floating
But I do not know where the tide will take me

The Entertainer

He spends an age readying himself
The stage has standards
And he has a role to fill
He oftentimes wonders
If people appreciate him
Or his craft

He does not remember the last time he was seen
Without makeup
And without embellishment
An audience awaits him
And they expect a performance

He must go

The Little Things

I search for melody in the mundane
I find interest in the world's intricacies
Like tyre marks in the dirt
Or dewdrops on the window pane

I am captivated by stars
I find the hubbub of the world deterring
And the speed of life jarring
I care not for capitalists and their cars

I do not need your money
I favour whimsy
And the little things
I guess that makes me funny

What Are You After?

To what do I owe the pleasure
Of a minute of your time?
You've never shared it before
So why the sudden change?

I sense a motive
Do not lie
I'm in demand when I have purpose
When I'm dormant I'm solitary

What benefit am I giving you?
And what are you giving me?

Oh dear –
Looks like my minute is up

Tick Tock

Time Changes
Time Heals
Does it?
My Time does nothing
And I do nothing with my Time
It's there but I don't sense it
Yet it has a hold over me

Flowers and War
Don't Mix

Flower children beware
Your dream has wilted
Your visions of a pacifist paradise
Lie like cacti in the marsh

What use are your petals to combat the blast?
You stand behind irradiated stems
And still believe people can change
War will always be the default option
And we consent to its havoc

Your serene utopia will not come to pass
Your ideas are to be admired
But they are not realistic
And it is time for you to face facts
As we have done already

Keep Running

I am on the heels of a good time
I have chased this feeling for so long
And I can almost reach out and grab it
I am aware of the despair at my back
But I have outrun it for so long already
And even when it caught me
I was able to escape
I sense freedom
So onward I charge

The Day You Left

The sun dimmed
And the world lost its wonder
The day you left

Everything became so empty
And I've never known such quiet until
The day you left

I've tried and tried
To banish this melancholy I've held since
The day you left

But nothing has felt the same
And I can trace it back to
The day you left

Shell

A soul that is hollow and a heart that is broken
A head full of words that will remain unspoken
A lifetime has been claimed by hurt and sorrow
And a false hope that you will be there
tomorrow

My tears have learnt to spell your name
I weep for a life that won't be the same
What was the last thing on your mind,
As you left this mortal realm behind?

Did your mind drift to me?
Because you're all that I can see
Distractions fail and no matter what I do
I find that my thoughts will always turn to you

How does a person become a memory?
If joy is wealth, then I'm in beggary
I've always wondered what more I could have
done
Then maybe I wouldn't be sat here so glum

I think of you everyday and despair
That I come home and you're not there

I hope that one day we will meet again
But I will live half empty until then

It's Easier to Stay Inside

I think I'll stay in
Because it looks cold outside
And maybe it'll rain

There doesn't seem to be any wind
But it looks cold outside
And what if it rains?

The sky is only slightly grey
But it looks cold outside
And what if it rains?

Yes, I have a coat nearby
But what if it's too cold
And there's too much rain?

I'll go out tomorrow
If it's not cold
And it doesn't rain

Familiar

It's strange how comfortable I've become with
misery
It's like second nature to me
It makes a change from crippling numbness

Just once I'd like a good day
I don't remember what one feels like
But I'd be sure to greet it like an old friend
And welcome it inside to reminisce about the
past

We'd discuss the immaterial and the profound
And it would bring me joy
To know that I've reached success

I'd bid them a fond farewell, confident I'd be
seeing them again
But we have not yet become acquainted
And it is a meeting I long for

9 789357 444798